ESSAY BOOK PART-1

IMPORTANT ENGLISH ESSAY FOR STUDENTS

RAJEE

This book is dedicated to all students who strive for excellence in their studies, to teachers who guide them with patience and wisdom, and to parents who encourage them to achieve their dreams. May this book be a source of knowledge and inspiration for all.

Contents

I
Myself

① *My name is Junaid.*

② *I am nine years old.*

③ *I live in Mumbai.*

④ *My school name is A.B.C.*

⑤ *I study in class 3.*

⑥ *My favourite subject is English.*

⑦ *I am strong and healthy.*

⑧ *My hobby is playing cricket.*

⑨ *I have one brother.*

⑩ *I want to become a doctor.*

II
My Mother

① *My mother's name is Deepti.*

② *She is a housewife.me*

③ *She is very kind and humble.*

④ *She is a very hardworking woman.*

⑤ *She takes care of everyone in my family.*

⑥ *She gets up early in the morning.*

⑦ *She loves cooking and gardening.*

⑧ *She is my first teacher.*

⑨ *She teaches me discipline and moral values.*

⑩ *My mother is the best mother in the world.*

III
My Father

① *My father's name is Pritam.*

② *He is my real hero.*

③ *He is forty years old.*

④ *He is a teacher.*

⑤ *My father is very kind and helpful.*

⑥ *He helps me in my studies.*

⑦ *He teaches me good habits.*

⑧ *He loves all family members.*

⑨ *He is everything for me.*

⑩ *I love him very much.*

IV
My School

① *My school name is B.M. School.*

② *It is an english medium school.*

③ *My school is near my house.*

④ *My school is the best school of my city.*

⑤ *My school building is very big and beautiful.*

⑥ *My school has a big playground.*

⑦ *There is a computer lab and a big library.*

⑧ *All teachers of my school are very kind and helpful.*

⑨ *I learn new things everyday in my school.*

⑩ *I love my school very much.*

V
My Best Friend

① *Aryan is my best friend.*

② *He is my classmate.*

③ *He is ten years old.*

④ *My best friend is very kind.*

⑤ *He is very good in studies.*

⑥ *We play together at school.*

⑦ *He always supports me in trouble.*

⑧ *He respects teachers and elders.*

⑨ *He is honest, caring and smart.*

⑩ *I feel lucky to have him.*

VI
My Family

① *I have a wonderful family.*

② *My family is a small family.*

③ *There are four members in my family.*

④ *They are my father, mother, me and my brother.*

⑤ *My father is a doctor.*

⑥ *My mother is a housewife.*

⑦ *We live together very happily.*

⑧ *We are always ready to help each other.*

⑨ *My family members are very caring and supportive.*

⑩ *I love my family very much.*

VII
My Favourite Teacher

① *My favourite teacher is Mrs. Lily.*

② *She teaches us Science.*

③ *She is an ideal teacher.*

④ *She teaches very well.*

⑤ *She explains everything in simple words.*

⑥ *She is kind and very helpful*

⑦ *She encourages us to study well.*

⑧ *She makes learning fun and easy.*

⑨ *She treats everyone with respect.*

⑩ *I am very proud of my teacher.*

VIII
My Favourite Season

① Winter is my favourite season.

② It is a cold season.

③ It starts from November.

④ It ends in February.

⑤ It is a pleasant season.

⑥ I love wearing warm woolen clothes.

⑦ It is a season of fruits and vegetables.

⑧ I feel very active in Winter.

⑨ I enjoy playing outside with friends.

⑩ Winter is the best for me.

IX

Honesty Is The Best Policy

① *Honesty always brings trust and respect.*

② *People like those who speak truth.*

③ *Lies create problems in our life.*

④ *Honest people feel happy and free.*

⑤ *Truth makes relationships strong and pure.*

⑥ *Dishonesty leads to guilt and fear.*

⑦ *Honesty helps us gain good friends.*

⑧ *It makes life simple and peaceful.*

⑨ *Being honest builds a good character.*

⑩ *Honesty is the best policy forever.*

X
My Hobby

① *My hobby is reading books.*

② *Reading books is a very good habit.*

③ *Reading books gives us a lot of knowledge.*

④ *I read many types of books.*

⑤ *Reading can improve our speaking skills also.*

⑥ *I very much enjoy reading.*

⑦ *I read books atleast two hours in a day.*

⑧ *It is like a fun for me.*

⑨ *In fact reading is best for me.*

⑩ *I like my hobby very much.*

XI
My Favourite Animal

① *My favourite animal is dog.*

② *Dog is a pet animal.*

③ *It looks very cute.*

④ *It is a four-footed animal.*

⑤ *It has two eyes, two ears and a tail.*

⑥ *It is a very faithful animal.*

⑦ *Dogs are found in white, black, and brown colours.*

⑧ *Dog's teeth are very sharp.*

⑨ *Its body is hairy.*

⑩ *I love spending time with a dog.*

XII
My House

① My house is very beautiful.

② There are four rooms in my house.

③ There are many doors and windows in my house.

④ There is a good kitchen in my house.

⑤ I live in my own house with my family.

⑥ There is a beautiful garden outside my house.

⑦ Sunlight and fresh air come from all sides in my house.

⑧ My house is always clean.

⑨ We feel very safe in the house.

⑩ I like my house very much.

XIII
Republic Day

① *Republic Day is a great day.*

② *It is celebrated on 26th January.*

③ *It is our national festival.*

④ *It is a very proud day for us.*

⑤ *Our constitution came into force on 26th January 1950.*

⑥ *The constitution is the supreme law of India.*

⑦ *We must respect our constitution.*

⑧ *The President of India hoists the national flag.*

⑨ *It is celebrated with joy.*

⑩ *Republic Day teaches us to live in unity and peace.*

XIV
Mobile Phone

①　*Mobile phone is an electronic device.*

②　*It has made our life easier.*

③　*It is also known as smartphone.*

④　*Mobile phone is very useful.*

⑤　*We can call friends and family.*

⑥　*It allows us to send messages.*

⑦　*We use it for online learning.*

⑧　*We can listen to music anytime.*

⑨　*Too much use is not good.*

⑩　*We should use it wisely always.*

XV
Diwali

① *Diwali is a famous hindu festival.*

② *Diwali is the festival of lights.*

③ *It comes in October or November.*

④ *On this day, Lord Rama came back from exile.*

⑤ *We clean our house on Diwali.*

⑥ *We decorate our house with diyas.*

⑦ *We make rangoli in our house.*

⑧ *At night we worship Goddess Lakshmi.*

⑨ *It is the festival of joy and happiness.*

⑩ *Diwali marks the victory of light over darkness.*

XVI

A Visit to a Zoo

① *Last Sunday, I visited the zoo.*

② *Many animals were there to see.*

③ *Lions, tigers and bears looked strong.*

④ *Monkeys jumped and played with joy.*

⑤ *Elephants were eating grass and bananas.*

⑥ *Birds were singing in their cages.*

⑦ *The crocodiles were resting in water.*

⑧ *I clicked pictures of many animals.*

⑨ *It was a fun and educational trip.*

⑩ *I enjoyed my visit a lot!*

XVII
A Pen

① **A pen is used for writing.**

② **It has ink inside for work.**

③ **Students use pens in their school.**

④ **Many colours of pens are available.**

⑤ **A pen helps us write neatly.**

⑥ **Some pens are black or blue.**

⑦ **A pen is small and light.**

⑧ **We can buy pens in shops.**

⑨ **People sign documents with pen.**

⑩ **A pen is a great tool.**

XVIII
Good Habits

① *Get up early in the morning.*

② *Brush your teeth twice a day.*

③ *Take a bath everyday.*

④ *Exercise regularly.*

⑤ *Eat healthy foods.*

⑥ *Don't waste food and water.*

⑦ *Wash your hands before and after meal.*

⑧ *Study regularly.*

⑨ *Always respect your elders.*

⑩ *Always speak the truth.*

XIX
Cat

① Cat is a pet animal.

② It is a small animal.

③ It has four legs.

④ It has two eyes and two ears.

⑤ It has a tail.

⑥ It loves to eat milk and fish.

⑦ It looks like a tiger club.

⑧ Its teeth are very sharp.

⑨ Its body is hairy and soft.

⑩ I have a cat in my home.

XX
Apple

① *Apple is a fruit.*

② *It is red in colour.*

③ *It is sweet in taste.*

④ *It has small seeds in it.*

⑤ *It is rich in vitamin C and fibre.*

⑥ *It is very good for our health.*

⑦ *It is used to make juice, jelly, jam etc.*

⑧ *It is grown in hilly areas.*

⑨ *We should eat an apple everyday.*

⑩ *Apple is my favourite fruit.*

XXI
My Pet Dog

① *I have a pet dog.*

② *Its name is Shera.*

③ *It is white in colour.*

④ *It lives in kennel.*

⑤ *It barks loudly.*

⑥ *It runs very fast.*

⑦ *I give him roti, milk and bread.*

⑧ *It protects our house.*

⑨ *It is very faithful animal.*

⑩ *I like my dog very much.*

XXII
Mango

① *Mango is a very tasty fruit.*

② *Mango is our national fruit.*

③ *It is the king of all fruits.*

④ *It comes in the summer season.*

⑤ *There are many types of mangoes.*

⑥ *It is sweet and sour in taste.*

⑦ *It is used to make pickle, jam, juice etc.*

⑧ *It is rich in vitamin A and C.*

⑨ *It is very good for our health.*

⑩ *I like mango very much.*

XXIII
Peacock

① *Peacock is a beautiful bird.*

② *It has two legs.*

③ *Its neck is long.*

④ *It has two small eyes.*

⑤ *It has blue feathers.*

⑥ *It has crown on its head.*

⑦ *It dances in rainy season.*

⑧ *It lives in garden and forest.*

⑨ *It eats fruits, grains and insects.*

⑩ *It is the national bird of India.*

XXIV
Tiger

① *Tiger is a wild animal.*

② *Tiger is our national animal.*

③ *Tiger lives in the forest.*

④ *It has a strong body.*

⑤ *Tiger's body is striped.*

⑥ *It has four legs, two eyes and a tail.*

⑦ *It has very sharp teeth and nails.*

⑧ *Tiger is a carnivorous animal.*

⑨ *Tiger runs very fast.*

⑩ *Tiger belongs to the cat family.*

XXV
The Sun

① *The Sun is a star.*

② *The Sun gives us light.*

③ *The Sun is a ball of fire.*

④ *It gives us heat.*

⑤ *It is the centre of our solar system.*

⑥ *It rises in the East in the morning.*

⑦ *It sets in the West in the evening.*

⑧ *Plants need sunlight to grow.*

⑨ *Without Sun there is no life on the Earth.*

⑩ *So I like the Sun very much.*